Can Reb Win?

By Sally Cowan

Lots of kids can hip hop.

Reb can hip hop, too!

But can Reb win
the Hip Hop Cup?

Mum got a big tub.

It had a lid.

Mum got the lid off.

Reb can see lots of wigs in the tub.

Reb got a big wig.

Reb did lots of hip hop!

Rib the rat did hip hop, too!

Reb got her wig.

She got her cap.

Rib got his kit!

Lots of kids can see Reb.

Reb did hip hop!

Can Reb win?

Reb wins the Hip Hop Cup!

CHECKING FOR MEANING

1. What sort of dancing does Reb like to do? *(Literal)*

2. What did Reb get out of the tub? *(Literal)*

3. How might Reb have felt before the hip hop competition? *(Inferential)*

EXTENDING VOCABULARY

lid	The word *lid* means a removable cover for a container. What has a lid in the story? What have you used a lid for?
wig	Look at the word *wig*. Find a word in the text that has *wig* as the base. What was added to the base to make the new word?
she	Look at the word *she*. What sound does it start with? What letters make the sound?

MOVING BEYOND THE TEXT

1. Do you like hip hop? Why or why not?

2. What other types of dance are there?

3. What do you have to do to be good at dancing?

4. Reb won the Hip Hop Cup. What other events have trophies as prizes?

SPEED SOUNDS

Kk	Ll	Vv	Qq	Ww
Dd	Jj	Oo	Gg	Uu

Cc	Bb	Rr	Ee	Ff	Hh	Nn
Mm	Ss	Aa	Pp	Ii	Tt	

PRACTICE WORDS

lid

win

kit

wig

lots

wigs

Lots

wins

kids